Singing My Sister to Sleep: LifeSongs

MOIRA KNEER

HELEN GIERKE

Published by Life Sister Songs, LLC
Cape Coral FL
2014

First Printing: 2014

ISBN 978-1-4675-9579-7

Life Sister Songs LLC
1620 Orchid Boulevard
Cape Coral, Florida 33904
www.lifesistersongs.com

Additional copies of this book and supplemental study materials may be ordered through the website.

Ordering Information:
Special discounts are available on quantity purchases by corporations, associations, educators, and others. For details, contact the publisher at the above listed address.

U.S. trade bookstores and wholesalers: Please contact Life-SisterSongs, LLC Tel: (239) 898-0945; or email hgierke@lifesistersongs.com

Singing My Sister to Sleep: LifeSongs

Dedications

Singing My Sister to Sleep could not have happened without the sister that I sang songs to so many nights as we grew up, often in a new place, trying to fit in.

When I used to help with orientation for new colleagues at Sacred Heart Hospital, I always told them this story to help them remember that we never know how we touch the lives of other people.

"I have one sibling, my younger sister Helen. She is very smart and talented. She is a wonderful musician, plays piano and organ and flute and piccolo! She sings and writes music and directs choirs. She has even written a book! I am not a musician, I cannot play any musical instrument and I am nowhere as smart as she is. When she was in school working on her Doctorate in Liturgical Studies and Theology, she told me about giving a presentation to a large group of musicians and educators. When I asked her if she was worried, she stunned me with her reply. 'No,' she said. 'I don't get nervous. I just pretend I'm you. You always look confident and competent.' So you see, you never know how other people see you."

For whatever reason, she sees me that way. For that I thank her and without her I wouldn't have attempted to write this book, to tell these stories, to offer our LifeSongs. You are my precious sister and I thank God for you.

Moira Kneer

To my big sister, who taught me to read, to sing, and to love and embrace life, whatever it may bring. Sing it, sister!

Helen Gierke

Contents

Preludes

Moira

It's a little before 5:00 a.m. and the sun is already shining, promising another sweltering Midwest summer day. From seemingly nowhere, a phrase comes to my mind...singing my sister to sleep.

I haven't thought about that in a long time. She's fast approaching her 62nd birthday, and mine has long since passed, but that's what I used to do—sing my sister to sleep. When we were little kids (me older by five years) and moved to a new city as we followed Dad in his military service, my singing would help her to get to sleep. Now, I'm no opera singer or diva of any sort. I just am able, or was able in my younger years, to memorize the words to almost any song. So I'd sing church choir songs, or popular songs, or old time songs...whatever she wanted me to sing.

For several years it was the more forgettable songs of Broadway musicals. The more obscure, the better my sister liked them. During our nightly chore of dishwashing and drying, the kitchen became our concert hall. We went through the Jeanette McDonald and Nelson Eddy operettas. (When she got older and learned the songs, I was Nelson to her Jeanette.)

Sometimes we would link songs: One person sings up to a certain word and then the other person has to start a different song with that word. (Who knew that would become known as "throw downs" 50 years later, in movies like *Pitch Perfect*!) We sang Broadway shows, rock and roll, folk—anything was fair game.

But still, at night, she would ask and I would sing. After she fell asleep I would dream about all the wonderful things I would do when I grew up. I would fantasize about finally living in one place and not having to move every year or so.

I was the "new kid" in fifteen different schools from kindergarten to college. During roll call on the first day, I could tell when the teacher was coming to my name because she always paused, squinted a bit, and then mangled my name.

I learned as an adult that "Moira" is a very popular name in Ireland. To this day there is only one other person I have met with that name. So right away, things would be off to an awkward start. One third grade teacher (I had two) actually asked me if I didn't mean Myra? I assured her that I was pretty certain I knew my real name, and it was not Myra, or Maria, or Mara.

When I went home at the end of the day, I knew not to mention these encounters. If Mom had had her way, I would have been called Sister like all the little girls in southern families. But we didn't always live in the South, and usually the only people called Sister were the nuns who taught in whatever Catholic schools my folks could find on our journeys.

This was ironic because I had actually been named for one of my father's sisters who was a real Sister—a Benedictine nun who had taken the name of Sister Moira. My folks had great hopes that one day I, too, would "take the veil." But by the time I was in high school, Sisters were leaving the convents in droves. Nobody was choosing the celibate life.

In high school I was still singing my sister to sleep, usually with music contest pieces that were just a little too high for my contralto voice. One was an early 20th century, nearly Victorian piece titled *Sing Me to Sleep*. She just loved that one, even if the words were dark and the reference was not to sleep but to death and dying.

Strangely enough, she was the music talent in the family. She excelled at the piano, then the flute, the organ, and any other instrument she got her hands on. She sang, wrote music, directed choirs, repaired instruments, and eventually earned a Master's in Sacred Music and a Doctorate in liturgical studies and theology. She was looking through her treasure trove of old music a few years ago and found the sheet music to *Sing Me to Sleep*. Funny, I had totally forgotten the song – although she never had – until she played it for me. She had such fond memories of when her big sister would sing her to sleep.

Sing me to sleep, the shadows fall,
let me forget the world and all.
Tired is my heart, the day is long;
would it were come to evensong.
                    (Clifton Bingham and Edwin Greene, 1910)

Helen

Okay, so I was a pest. On hot, muggy nights in Florida, falling asleep was nearly impossible.

We lived in Miami and Jacksonville from the time I was about three or four until...well, off and on until I was 14. Early on, the only air conditioner was a room-sized one in my parents' bedroom, reserved for only the stickiest of nights.

Moira and I shared a room and a double bed with a mattress that was pretty thin and every move one person made was felt by the other. A double bed is not very big, even for kids, and the stored-up heat from a day in the sun would radiate from each of us, seeming to multiply and driving the temperature even higher. So we would open the windows, try to tune out the crickets and frogs, listen to the small fan as it stirred the hot air around, and hope for a cool breeze. Flip the pillow. Turn over. Take off the sheet. Flip the pillow. Sigh. "Sing me a song, Moira."

"Go to sleep."

"It's too hot. Sing me a song, just one."

Sigh. "Which one?"

"I don't care."

I could almost hear her paging through songs in her mind, and then she'd sing. Sometimes she would put her hand on the top of my head, I think to make me be still, and I would listen and fall asleep, at least for a while. I would often wake up later, crawl out of bed and lie on the vinyl tile floor, cooler now in the *night, and very quietly sing to myself.*

I told her not long ago that the word that best described my childhood was "loneliness." I didn't know it at the time, of course, but I lived in my own little world of books and music until junior high. Despite the occasional feeling of despair, it was a pretty nice world in many ways.

Moira always wanted to play school, with me as the student, so I learned to read by 4 years of age, and I was a library rat from early on. We moved from Miami to Jacksonville late in my first grade year, and the school wasn't quite sure what to do with me at that point. The very nice teacher (whose name I don't remember at all) pointed me to the library shelves in the room and left me to my own devices. That summer I attended the first of four or five annual summer reading programs sponsored by the local library. I must have read 65 books that first summer, setting the pattern for each summer to follow. The reward for being among the top readers was a trip to the local fire ranger tower, and I went every year. I felt like Smokey the Bear and I were friends on a first-name basis. We would shake Smokey's furry hand, climb up and down the tower, and sing the "Smokey the Bear" song. "With a ranger's hat and shovel and a pair of dungarees," is still in the jukebox in my head.

Second grade brought Moira, our brother George (two years older than she), and me to the same Catholic school. She was so pretty and smart and popular, and being five years behind her, I felt nothing but awe. She and George were encouraged to join the choir. Apparently, George's (at that time undiagnosed) ADHD was causing some disruption, and our parents were "invited" to join the choir as well—for supervision of the "young'uns." Choir practice was held on a weeknight, and since I couldn't be left home alone, I was brought along, too.

Small for my age, I mostly lurked on the back bench and watched and listened. Sometimes I snuck over to the organ, where Mrs. H. was the accompanist. She was kind and let me watch her feet and sometimes sit by her on the bench. The mysterious writing that scrolled above the words was so intriguing!

We sang in Latin, of course, from the St. Gregory's Hymnal. Mr. Brown, the director, was an extraordinarily patient man. He had studied at the Sorbonne and was married to a French woman who was, of course, beautiful and blonde. When the (even to my young ears) terrible tenors sang, he would kind of crinkle up his eyes. I could see the pain. I took to singing the tenor part softly in the ear of the worst singer of the section, and actually helped. Mr. Brown smiled at me. I thought, "That has to be the best job ever." I loved the Latin, the way the parts wound around each other, the solidity of the bass line that my father sang. I'm not sure how long Moira and George lasted, but Mom and Dad—and little tag-along—sang in the choir until we moved.

I began piano lessons with Mrs. H. when I was seven. I would bike over to her house on Saturday morning and play for at least an hour, far longer than the lesson fee allowed. Then, more often than not, I would stay and help her hang her laundry on the clothesline and have a little lunch with her. She let me talk, she answered questions, we sang sometimes—she was like a grandmother to me. We didn't have a piano at home, so she encouraged me to practice on the table top, imagining the keys and the sounds. I know I irritated a lot of teachers doing that on my desk in school, too. But it worked.

Learning to read music was like learning to read books. Any piece was fair game to my deciphering and devouring mind. Every song went into the jukebox in my head. Whether it was a ukulele (Moira got one, and I quickly abducted it), a toy accordion that came from somewhere, or the school piano, I wanted to learn it, to play it, to sing with it.

> Love, I am lonely, years are so long.
> I want you only, you and your song.

We grew up and each had our own families. Mom and Dad dragged me to northern Wisconsin, where I finished a music education degree, got married, and started having kids, three boys. Pregnant with my first son during my college years, I jokingly said he went to more concerts before he was born than most people do in their entire lives. Even in utero he would kick in time to Mozart. He didn't much like Chopin, though.

At home Chris and I sang and danced and listened to every kind of record I could buy, beg or borrow. Dad had given me the old record player/radio, a piece of furniture that was actually pretty sophisticated for its vintage. It even had treble and bass controls that Chris, as soon as he could walk, learned to adjust to suit his own very particular ears.

Eventually we moved to a small town in northern Wisconsin, where I was hired as the choir director at a local Lutheran church. Expecting my second son, I was quite a sight at Easter: eight months pregnant and balancing on a step-stool so the choir could see me. I taught piano and other music lessons, often with a baby or small child on my lap. One of the special gifts of small towns is that no one really minded.

Church choirs develop a special relationship, a closeness that is family. When crises, tragedies, or difficulties occur (as they always do), the members are supportive and "there" for one another. When my third son was born, they celebrated with me. When my marriage ended, they mourned with me.

I was there for nearly 10 years. During that time six of "my" choir members died. We sang at every funeral. Two got married, and we sang at their weddings. When I remarried, they sang at my wedding. When I finally moved away, we all cried together. Another song in the symphony of my life began.

Moira

Yes, we grew up and each had our own families. When we got together there were seven kids between us! And they fit like doorsteps! On one of the rare times we could get together, the kids were Jenny, 11; Cathy, 10; Christopher, 9; Steven, 7; Nicole, 6; Greg, 5; and Daniel, 3. What a collection!

During those hectic yet precious years I would sing my own kids to sleep. We sang silly songs, lullabies, counting songs, popular songs. I knew lots of camp songs, so we sang about PUFF, the Magic Dragon, and the Hole in the Bottom of the Sea, and Michael Rowing his Boat Ashore. We sang dreamer songs about the Big Rock Candy Mountain. When the two oldest were still in diapers they would sing songs from Jesus Christ Superstar, shocking the older ladies in K-Mart as they lisped, "Jesus Cwist, Jesus Cwist, who are you what have you sac-wificed?"

To this day I believe that is the real reason my second daughter got hooked on hard rock.

We also sang selected numbers from *Hair*, heavily censored by me!

The two younger kids were pressed into service when their older sisters needed bodies for the plays they invariably put on. Times were hard, and entertainment was what you made of it! We struggled for a while, and it was difficult to sing anyone to sleep without tears. Type I Juvenile diabetes struck the two youngest girls at the tender ages of 2 and 7. It took a toll on my marriage. We supported one another, the kids and I, with our songs and our imaginations.

I listened to songs in my head while I sat in doctors' waiting rooms, in lab waiting rooms, in hospital waiting rooms. I would try to remember lyrics to keep myself awake through bedside vigils when one or the other of them experienced some of the many complications of childhood diabetes. I even found myself playing our song game in my head...singing a song, taking the last word and starting a new song.

It seems like I have always sung in the choir. From those first years with Mom and Dad, in schools as we moved from town to town, and as an adult in the church choir, it was a fundamental part of my life. It also gave me time to reflect on God's presence in my life. St. Augustine said, "Singing is praying twice." My prayers often consisted of singing psalms from church hymnals. During those years, singing kept me sane.

After my divorce it quickly became apparent that I was going to have to supplement our meager child support income. I started working in the school lunch program at the parochial school my children attended. I could take the kids to school, give the two girls their insulin, check their blood sugars and be there when school was over. Eventually the pastor invited me to complete a course in Youth Ministry certification, and I was hired as the parish Youth Minister.

I threw myself into the job! We went on winter campouts,

created our own retreat days, and participated in the large youth gatherings and encounter experiences. I told my faith story and really rejoiced in the chance to bring young people a glimpse of the wonder I had experienced. The youth group kids liked me to tell them what they called "Moira Stories" about living in other places, feeling like I didn't fit in but finding something inside of myself. About beginning to know God.

I met my new spouse at church...singing in the choir! Where else? We sang together and eventually, as the kids put it, we all got married.

I still sang my kids to sleep once in a while, but they were growing up, moving out, and spreading their wings, each with his or her own set of gifts and challenges. My oldest daughter was the brave one, the bold one, the bright shining light. She worked her way through college, graduated with a degree in education, and eventually secured a good job in a small town not too far away. She married and produced my first grand-child. I loved to sing that precious little girl to sleep when I could.

My second daughter graduated and bought a house! She, too, worked her way through school. But juvenile diabetes was ravaging her body. Her eyesight was diminishing at an alarm-ing rate. Laser treatments didn't help. More and more expensive and complicated treatment and surgeries failed to halt the rush to darkness. By the time she had lost most of her sight, her overall health was becoming precarious. Her caustic doctor of the moment delivered the harsh message, "If you don't have a pancreas transplant in the next year, you'll be dead in five years!" Then he left the room.

She turned to me and said, "Mom, I didn't do this! I didn't ask for this! It's not my fault!" It was harsh news for someone not yet thirty. So we began a strange journey that took us to the terrifying but lifesaving world of transplants. Cathy secured a place on the transplant list. University of Minnesota-Fairview was one of the few hospitals actually doing pancreas transplants. She even changed jobs so that she would have good medical insurance. I remember so well getting the call at one o'clock in the morning, that they had a pancreas for her. We had six hours to get to the hospital two hours away.

Little did I know that we would be there for nearly a month. Pancreas transplants were very new and risky. We couldn't know then that the long term success rate was only 40%. Cathy received her organ from a cadaver donor in 1999. We also didn't know that the anti-rejection drugs that made her so sick would accelerate the destruction of her kidneys. Within two years we were at the Mayo Clinic in Rochester, Minnesota, where she was undergoing testing for a kidney transplant.

As I sat in the waiting room, knowing that it was <u>my</u> son giving part of his body, his kidney, to his sister, I didn't know if I could ever sing again. After a while, you go on autopilot...the prayers come, you still breathe, but you don't know how you can keep it up, keep it going, turn the next page. You just do. So, through the pancreas transplant, kidney transplant, loss of sight...still we managed to sing. Sing the newest grandbaby to sleep. Sing myself to sleep.

During the time of waiting for the pancreas transplant I was working as part of the parish pastoral team, assisting the pastor in most areas of parish life. I kept going to school, learning more and more about successful parishes, what people were looking for, and digging deeper into my own personal faith life. About a year after the pancreas transplant I decided to quit the field instead of struggling against the tide that was changing at my parish. I took a couple of interim positions...one with the Benedictine Sisters and another with a local women's advocacy agency.

In the last years of parish work I had collaborated with the stewardship consultant hired by the church. We shared ideas, and he invited me to speak to other churches that were embarking on similar building projects. My area of expertise was volunteer ministries, recruitment, and retention. The owner of the consultancy firm invited me to consider working full time for him. It would mean travel, but I would have more control over my time so I agreed. I became a Road Warrior! I traveled over three states, working with churches of all denominations, and even secular non-profits, giving workshops, guiding committees, selling dreams.

During this very difficult time, my son offered one of his

kidneys to my daughter Cathy. My job gave me the freedom to be with her, to work from our hotel room during the month I lived in Rochester at Mayo Clinic. I was so grateful to my employer and to the God who guided me to that place. I sang as I drove, playing my favorite CDs, thanking God for his care, asking his protection for me and my loved ones.

My youngest daughter, Nicole, diagnosed with Type I diabetes at age 2, never knew any other way of living...always checking blood sugars, watching her diet, forgoing the candy at Halloween, the Christmas goodies, the Kool-Aid and soft drinks before artificial sweetener. She started drinking coffee at age five! Her favorite treat was cottage cheese.

Her diabetes was severe but better controlled. She married a very nice young man who took all her health issues in stride. When her first child was born almost two months premature she didn't panic. I worried when she became pregnant again very soon after. This baby, too, was born early and spent the first few weeks of his life in the Neonatal unit...a big baby compared to most preemies.

Mothers with diabetes have bigger babies.

My heart went out to her when this younger son was four and his difficult behavior prompted her to check his blood sugar. He, too, began his life with Type I diabetes. "Mom," she asked with tears in her eyes, "is he going to hate me because he has diabetes?"

"O honey, I don't think so. Do you hate me?" She looked at

me incredulously, "Why would I hate you? It's not your fault." And neither was it hers.

It was only about a year later that I remember waking up wide awake, hours before my regular time, with the words to the hymn *Eye Has Not Seen* running through my head:

Our lives are but a single breath,
We flower and we fade;
Yet all our days are in your hands,
So we return in love what love has made.

(Marty Haugen © 1982, GIA Publications)

Where had that come from, I wondered. An hour later the phone rang and Nicole called to tell me she was on the way to the hospital with heart pains. She was only 32! Could I come? Could I help with her boys?

I sang the psalms all the way on the two hour drive. I sang to the boys as I had sung to them since their premature births: nonsense songs, lullabies, tongue twisters, silly songs. For the oldest one, his favorite song, whatever the season, was *Silent Night*. He loved to hear the words "sleep in heavenly peace." I assured him that Mom was going to be all right. That God loved them. That all would be well. After angioplasty and surgery to place a stent in one of her arteries, she returned home to be nurtured and cherished by her family.

I went back on the road. I had been working for the company for five years, gaining priceless experience dealing with people, encouraging religious communities in trusting God's plan for them, and challenging whole congregations to step out in faith. I often spoke (with understandable pride) of my son and daughter's transplant journey, telling the story of his love and generosity, of her trust and bravery, to inspire faith, courage, and generosity in others.

I arrived home late one night from a church presentation on the other side of the state. I was tired and immediately went to bed. About 3 am I woke up, feeling clammy and cold, nauseated and breathless. Wondering if I was coming down with the flu I went into the bathroom. As I looked at my pale face in the mirror, it finally dawned on me: I had all the symptoms of a heart attack! I had been carrying nitro medication for years, sometimes forgetting I even had it.

I woke my husband up and told him I was having a heart attack. In the typical response for most women, I said I did not want an ambulance. The rationale: what if I'm not? I'll feel foolish.

When we arrived at the hospital, I went off to the heart cath (short for catheterization) lab where the doctors could take a closer look at my heart. An angiogram showed blockage in my heart, and I ultimately had a stent placed in the artery to open it up. Afterwards, we talked about how lucky it was that I had been at home, and wasn't driving when it happened, that I wasn't out of town overnight, and so forth.

The morning after I came home from the hospital, I was sitting at the kitchen table, drinking my now *decaffeinated* coffee, pondering my next move. As my husband so plainly put it, I would be tempting fate to continue my hectic travel schedule. I needed to do something else. All my life I had tried to do what God wanted. I blessed God for all the good things I had been given and ignored the hard things. I tried to serve others in His name, working for the church, working with churches, going the extra mile, volunteering when able, singing and singing and singing.

Suddenly I was yelling at the Lord! "What is it you want? What? I try to do everything you want, I never complained about the crosses you gave me. I tried to do the best I could. Well, whatever it is that you want me to do now, you'd better make it clear and plain. I cannot understand what this is all about so tell me in plain words what you want!" I even banged my cup down on the table for emphasis.

About five minutes after my tirade, the phone rang. I angrily checked the caller ID, not really wanting to talk to anyone at that point. The ID said the call was blocked. It could be my friend from the courthouse calling to check on me, as she often did. I grudgingly answered and heard this little voice on the line. "This is Sister Augusta Sperl from Sacred Heart Hospital. Do you remember me?" Taken aback, I recalled the tiny dynamo who ran the Pastoral Care Department at the local Catholic hospital.

"Yes, Sister, I remember you."

Never one to beat around the bush, Sister Augusta said,

"There is an opening for a chaplain in our Pastoral Care Department. I think you should come in and talk to me about working here."

OK. I took the phone away from my ear and eyed it incredulously. "Sister, I just had angioplasty," I said.

"Good, dear, you're recuperating. The job doesn't start for four weeks. You come in on Wednesday. Just ask for me." She hung up.

I immediately apologized to the Lord God. I thanked him for being clear and direct and also told him I certainly wasn't qualified to do this job, but yes, I'd go talk to Sister.

That began my eight-year career as a chaplain in a Level III acute care hospital. I came in by the back door, so to speak. I had spent years going to classes, attending workshops, and doing coursework in all areas of pastoral care. The Sisters wanted someone with academic training, but also with some life experience. I knew many of them and they knew my story.

Those eight years were a gift from God. There were many times when I found myself sitting at a bedside, holding a patient's hand, singing quietly as they waited...waited for God to come, waited to hear their diagnosis, waited to get better. I often thought of all the hours and days I had spent personally waiting in hospital rooms, in waiting rooms. I understood.

Singing my sister to sleep was great training. I have come to understand that the world is filled with LifeSongs, all fitting together in a vast cosmic symphony that is constantly being written by our Creator. Songs were sung by me, but also to me, for me, around me, and sometimes in spite of me. In the later hours of the evening shift at the hospital, after I wrote up my notes for the next chaplain, I would take a moment to note for myself some of the songs that I encountered in the many special people who walked through and in my life, some special message God had sent through a patient, a loved one, a hospital employee.

Moira's Songs

Part One

A Song of Humility

I could hardly believe it the first time I walked into a patient's room, announced that I was the chaplain and would be praying for that person while they were in the hospital and heard, "I don't really have time for this now. Just go away."

We aren't supposed to take it personally, but I did. It was hard for me to believe that I wouldn't be welcomed, or at least tolerated! But it wasn't the only time, and it wouldn't be the last.

That situation was quite different from the nice gentleman in the Critical Care Unit who, when I came to visit, nervously asked me if I knew any Lutheran prayers. His family kind of laughed, wondering if I was going to get upset. I gently assured him I could come up with a good Lutheran prayer, and we all had a laugh. People who pray over you sometimes are scary! It seems as if they have a special pass to access God, and who knows what they might say on my behalf. Even when a patient didn't want me to visit or stay, I would go to the chapel sometime during my shift and say a prayer for all those who did not yet know how much God loved them.

Blessed assurance, Jesus is mine!
O, what a foretaste of glory divine!

Fanny Crosby (1820-1915)

A Song of Encouragement

One of the most enjoyable parts of my job was visiting and praying with the dialysis patients who came for treatment three or four days a week. Over the years I grew very close to several of those special people who sit for four or five hours while machines cleanse their blood, doing the work for kidneys that don't function anymore. Some were like Richard, who loved to fish. He would leave from dialysis and go home for a nap so he could fish the next day. All during fishing season, every day he did not have dialysis he fished. He never complained about the treatment, only that it kept him from fishing every day.

As often as possible I told my daughter's success story, encouraging patients to consider or at least inquire about a kidney transplant. Quite a few of our patients did find donors and underwent successful transplants, joyfully giving up their chairs in the dialysis unit.

One of the special ones I'll call Judy made it her mission to brighten everyone's day: patients, technicians, nurses, social workers, chaplains or even the housekeeping crew. She collected recipes from everyone and published a "Dialysis Unit Cookbook," making copies for anyone interested. She wrote poetry for those folks who were having a bad time. She crocheted baby blankets for staff members who were pregnant. She had to lose 80 pounds to qualify for transplant, and she did it with a cheerful outlook. When she had recovered from the transplant surgery, she came back to encourage others.

A few years later Judy was diagnosed with cancer and underwent chemotherapy with lots of complications. Her usually cheerful outlook began to suffer under the rigors of her treatments. One day her devoted sister stopped me in the hall and asked if I could find a way to cheer Judy up. She had reached out to so many others; now she needed a special touch. I tried to think of a way to brighten her day.

I went to see her in her isolation room, asked how she was doing and listened as she listlessly responded. "Judy, I have a special favor to ask," I spoke hesitantly. Looking at me warily, she asked what it was.

"You wrote a special poem for the patients on this oncology floor. I saw it in the nurses' station. May I have your permission to have it published in the hospital newsletter? So many more people will see it and read it and it will bring hope and joy to everyone!"

She started to smile and said, "Well, of course you may! Are you sure it's good enough to go in the newsletter?" Everyone who came into the room for the rest of the week heard about her "publication," and the poem did indeed bring light into many other lives.

> *I am strong when I am on your shoulders,*
> *You raise me up to more than I can be.*
> (*You Raise Me Up*, Brendan Graham, b.1945)

A Song of Memories

Christine was in her early 80s, an elegant woman who was truly a "lady." She had sung in choirs all her life, and I would sing hymns with her, much to the delight of the other people in the dialysis unit. Whenever we sang we were joined by Arthur, another octogenarian who knew the words to every song anyone had ever heard. I once told him about my dear father-in-law, Bernie, another great songster. I told him how, when Bernie was dying, he asked me to sing with him. His favorite song was "The Man on the Flying Trapeze." I always claimed difficulty with the introduction, and he would sing for me:

> *Once I was happy but now I'm forlorn,*
> *Just like an old coat that is tattered and torn,*
> *Left in this wide world to weep and to mourn,*
> *Scorned by a girl in her teens!*
> *This lovely young maid she was handsome,*
> *And I tried all I knew her to please,*
> *But I could not please her one quarter so well*
> *As the man on the flying trapeze!*
>
> George Leybourne (1867)

That was the last song I sang for him and with him. How he loved to belt out the lines, "He flew through the air with the greatest of ease, that daring young man on the flying trapeze!" Arthur said Bernie probably saw himself as that romantic figure. And he said he understood. I can still see Bernie, then in his eighties, getting into his car, and going to the local nursing home to, as he put it, "visit the old people." Once a month, on birthday day, he would find the oldest lady having a birthday, put his arm around her in her wheelchair and sing "Let Me Call You Sweetheart." He always ended with a kiss. He made that lucky lady's special day even more memorable.

> *Let me call you "sweetheart," I'm in love with you,*
> *Let me hear you whisper that you love me too.*
> *Keep the lovelight glowing in your eyes so true;*
> *Let me call you "sweetheart", I'm in love with you!*
> Beth Slater Whitson (1910)

A Song of Hope

Some of my favorite nurses worked on the Behavioral Health floor. They are dedicated, compassionate commonsense people who have seen everything. When they would call I considered it a compliment that they asked for me.

One of those calls was in regard to a young woman whose significant other had brought her in for evaluation, saying, "She's being weird." Her nurse told me she was a very lovely young woman who needed someone to listen to her and give her some direction.

She was actually a beautiful girl who looked so sad. I introduced myself as the hospital chaplain and asked if there was anyone or anything special she wanted me to pray for. She tearfully asked if I would pray for her nine-month-old baby. "Tell me about her," I said. As she talked she became more animated, until she came to the part where she was separated from her daughter. I asked if she was married to the baby's dad.

"Oh, we're engaged, I guess. He said he wants to get married when he has time but, see, he has this farm and he works outside, too. He gets so mad at me when he comes home and supper's not ready."

After all she worked "only" part-time outside the home. And as her fiancé said, the baby sleeps a lot, so she should be able to cook and clean and take care of the garden. She had no sisters, no girl friends, and her mom was deceased. As I listened, I looked at this bright, beautiful young woman and started to get angry at what was happening. I had worked for a women's shelter; I knew what abusive behavior was.

"My dear young woman," I said, "if you could do anything you wanted, what would you like to do?" She immediately broke into a bright sunny smile and said, "I'd raise llamas."

What a surprise! I took her hand and told her what a wonderful person she was, a great loving mom, a talented and gifted woman who deserved the best and should not settle for anything less. I said, "This is what I'd tell you if you were my daughter: tell your boyfriend you want a ring and a wedding, or he can pay child support. Tell him you intend to raise llamas on the farm and want his support. Tell him to pick up his own clothes and treat you better, or you are leaving. Ask your doctor about post partum depression."

I gave her the number of the women's shelter and suggested she call them from the hospital, in case her "fiancé" didn't want to listen. I hugged her and went to talk to her nurse, Charlene, who was waiting to find out what I had said to her.

"You're just what she needed!" Charlene said. "With some patients, hearing this from medical staff makes the patient think they don't have a valid medical issue." The other nurses agreed that they had suspected some post partum depression. It might have been manageable, but without a support system she was slipping.

The staff had talked with the young man she lived with and felt he really was concerned, but focused too much on himself and his busy schedule. By the next afternoon when I came to work, she had already been discharged. I hope she is raising llamas.

I will come to you in the silence,
I will lift you from all your fear.
You will hear my voice, I claim you as my choice.
Be still and know I am here.

(*You Are Mine*, David Haas, © 1991 GIA)

A Song of Presence

At least once a day—and often more than that—I would hear the question, "Are you a Sister?" The Catholic hospital where I worked was established over 150 years ago by Franciscan nuns. Until about forty years ago the halls were filled with sisters in habits; administrators, nurses, technicians, therapists—you name it, and the sisters were filling the roles. In those short decades the numbers dwindled, until today there are only two sisters in the whole hospital, and they belong to another order!

So, when I came into a patient's room, wearing a cross and an ID tag that says "Chaplain," I would often hear the question, "Are you a Sister?" I would be tempted to say, "No, but my mother used to call me that."

Sometimes I would say, "No, but I can call one for you."

Other times I would simply explain that I am a lay woman serving as a chaplain.

When it seemed appropriate I would sometimes just say, "No, I am a grandma and a mom. I'm just a person like you who serves the hospital as a chaplain."

Some patients see the word chaplain and immediately feel threatened, anxious, or frightened.

"Am I that sick?? Do I need a chaplain? Do I need last rites or something?"

I tried to calm their fears with the reassurance that I visited everyone in the hospital. Then I'd ask a question about the care they were receiving or turn the conversation in a different direction.

At one time in my life I did think about becoming a Sister. There is a part of me that feels the call to the contemplative life...time to reflect, to praise God, to ponder the mysteries of life. But the other part usually wins. I love people. I love talking to folks and hearing their stories. I love my children, my husband, being married, running a home, having grandkids. I was the "church lady" in our local parish for many years, first as a Youth Minister, then as Pastoral Associate. My grandchildren would tell their friends that their Grandma is the Pray-er Lady: "She prays with people who don't feel good."

It is a blessing and privilege to be present when a family gathers for the death of a beloved mother or father. For a time, I am part of that family, present to help them walk through the lonesome valley—the valley of the shadow of death—and help them to overcome their fear. Jesus holds my hand and walks with me as I accompany them. How awe-some it is!

I may not be a Sister, but I am God's servant in the same way that the Sisters serve. It is my great joy to bring water to the thirsty and food to the hungry, and to visit the sick and those imprisoned by pain and fear and suffering. I thank God for the gift of this service.

Just a closer walk with thee,
Grant it, Jesus, is my plea.
Daily walking close to thee,
Let it be, dear Lord, let it be.
I am weak but thou art strong,
Jesus, keep me from all wrong.
I'll be satisfied as long as I walk,
Let me walk close to thee.

Anonymous

A Song of Unconditional Love

It's late at night. The afternoon shift ends at 11 pm. The hospital is quieter now, the lights have been lowered, and the daytime traffic of patients, visitors, and caregivers is gone. Patients for the most part are sleeping...or trying to. The cleaning people go quietly about their work. The main doors are locked, but anyone can enter through the emergency entrance.

Those doors are open all night. Security keeps watch during this busy time for the Emergency Room. The late-night car accidents, the chest pains that don't go away with bedtime, the lonely souls who feel they have nothing to live for—they come to the doors that are always open to them.

This is the hour when I will get a page for the mother in labor who really could use a prayer. Or the man who is facing prostate surgery tomorrow morning and just cannot sleep. Or maybe the cancer patient who cannot find surcease from her pain and just needs someone to talk to.

The night time is loaded with special needs, requests that we don't have time for in the busy daylight hours. Those hours are filled with tests and waiting, with walks and baths and waiting. With short visits or maybe no visits and waiting. The night is filled with fears, and allows too much time to ask the questions that we avoid in the busy bright daylight hours. Questions like, "What will the test show?"-- "What will they find with the surgery?"-- "Am I going to die?"-- "What's it like to die?"-- "Will I have pain?"--"What if it's cancer?"-- or maybe even, "What if it's not cancer?"

When they call, I come. I pull up a chair and listen. Sometimes I tell them a story. Sometimes I tell them about my fear, too, so they know they are not alone, that all of us have questions and fears. Sometimes I tell them about what I think God looks like. I tell them about Grandma God.

A poem by John Shea describes God as a comforting and comfortable grandmother. This is the image I hold of the Creator, the one who loves us unconditionally, who forgives us and takes us back and wraps us in a loving embrace. I can see her sitting in her celestial rocking chair. She invites us to climb up into her lap and rest our head on her ample bosom. As she rocks she rubs our back and tells us, "Don't worry. Don't cry. It's all gonna be okay. Grandma loves you." And for a minute all the fears, the worries, the anxiety goes away because we are safe in God's loving arms.

Be not afraid. I go before you always.
Come follow me, and I will give you rest.
    (Robert J. Dufford, SJ, © 1975, 1978 OCP Publications)

A Song of Hopefulness

She was a patient in the Critical Care unit. She had been found unresponsive, on the ground, in a little town a hundred miles north of where we live. The first responders transported her to the nearest local hospital. They evaluated her and transported her to our hospital for more acute care and treatment. She was on a ventilator, and it took time to locate her family.

As it turned out, she was the mother of seven children in a rural area. The father had left the family several years before. Victims of the Great Recession, he had lost his job, his hope, and his dignity.

He had not been able to pay child support, and the family eventually had to move out of their $500,000 home. They lived in a tent for a while, in the summer months. Mom dealt with a chronic disease that ate up their resources. Eventually they found a place in a trailer. The older kids had graduated from high school, gotten jobs and places to live so as not to be a burden to their mom.

Her medical condition was complicated by her many drug allergies, so she studied homeopathic healing. She was known as a Master Herbalist, treating her condition with natural products. She had been able to stay away from traditional health care for several years.

But the ravages of her disease caught up with her.

When she arrived at our hospital, her prognosis was poor.

Further testing showed that in her fall, she had sustained a head injury resulting in bleeding in the brain. Our physicians consulted with the nearest on-call neurosurgeon. Over the phone, he listened to the information we had and gave his opinion that there was nothing he would be able to do. He did not accept her as a patient. The hospital he was affiliated with preferred patients with insurance.

I was asked to speak to her children, to impress upon them the seriousness of their mother's condition.

It was one of the most difficult things I have ever done. I watched the oldest boy, only 23, as he held onto his younger brother and sister's hands while I told them that she could very well die, that there was little or no hope for recovery. "She's been sick before, but she's always pulled through," he said. "She's only 47."

"I know," I responded. "But you must prepare yourself and the other kids. Can you get them here? Do you need help?"

Reluctantly he told me he had no gas money, not even money for food for the day. When the nursing staff heard, they pooled their own personal resources and gave the family money for necessities. The oldest son fed his charges, made a call, and then asked if Mom would be okay for the night. He had to take the young ones to school and make arrangements to get the other kids here.

His mother died the next day, never having regained consciousness. I prayed that her family, her children, would find their way in a world that seemed to have little concern for them, for her. I prayed that they would know that the All Caring One was holding them in hands of love, and that other hands, human hands, would reach out to them and turn their song of hopelessness into hopefulness.

Jesus loves me this I know, for the Bible tells me so.
Little ones to him belong, they are weak but he is strong .
Yes, Jesus loves me, yes, Jesus loves me,
Yes, Jesus loves me, the Bible tells me so.

Anna Bartlett Warner (1862)

A Song of Mercy

I stopped at the information desk in the lobby of the hospital to ask a question and suddenly there was a young woman standing next to me, saying in a tearful voice, "Can you help me?"

"What do you need?" I asked.

"I'm looking for my boyfriend. I don't know what happened to him."

I asked her to tell me more. As she spoke, she continued to cry with utter despair. It seems that she and this young man had just moved to a small farming area about 80 miles away where he had taken a job as a laborer on a dairy farm. Her boyfriend was an eight-year veteran of the Iraq war who had become addicted to heroin. She also had a history of drug abuse, but they had decided to leave the area of Michigan they had lived in all their lives and start over, kicking the drug habit. She had been drug-free for almost a year.

They had only been in town a few days when he began to suffer severely from withdrawal, to the point that he asked her to call 911. She was frantic, and when the 911 operator informed her that the area they lived in wasn't served by 911 responders, she really panicked. She dialed the number of a local ambulance service. They arrived, loaded up her boyfriend, and told her they would transport him to the nearest health care facility that would take him both as a psych case and as an uninsured person.

She found his car keys and the next morning, with lots of directions from gas station attendants, found her way to our hospital. She did not know anyone. She arrived without money, without having eaten in two days, and quite literally at the end of her resources.

I explained to her that if he had been admitted as a psych patient the hospitals would not release information about him. She continued to sob silently. I checked our hospital and the other local hospitals without success. I was about to call facilities that were even further away when I thought about the rehab center located in the next town. I told her they might not even tell me if he was a patient and still she begged me to try. So I called giving my name and position as a Chaplain at Sacred Heart. I gave a brief history of the search and gave the young man's name and the girl's name. After a moment of silence, the voice on the other line said, please hold, which I did for another ten minutes. Finally the receptionist said she could tell us that he was there. He had given his girlfriend's name as the only person to release information to.

She physically collapsed when I told her we had found him. So I scooped her up, asked when she had eaten last, and hustled her off to the hospital cafeteria. She told me she was penniless and was so embarrassed about it. As Christians we are called to see the face of Christ in others. We are reminded in Matthew 25 that it is our responsibility to feed the hungry, to welcome the stranger, to comfort the afflicted.

I stuffed her pockets with food, gave her the little cash I had, and thought about what I could say to her to give her hope. As she ate her chicken noodle soup she told me that she had given birth three months before, but because of her drug background, the child had been taken away. Tearfully she confided that she had another child, a five-year-old, who was also in foster care. "This is my last chance," she said. "I am so afraid I will blow it."

Listening to my heart, I said to her, "Honey, we all make mistakes in our lives. We make bad choices. But that doesn't mean we are bad. You are a good person and God loves you. He made you, and he loves you. As much as you love your kids, God loves you more. He will not abandon you. Take one step at a time and hang on to the God who loves you so much."

It seemed impossible that this poor girl could have any more tears in her, but she did, and they poured out. "No one has ever told me that before. No one has ever said that I am a good person. I have done so many bad things."

We can all change. We can help one another if only we are willing to reach out, to listen, to put aside our fears and prejudices, and take the time. People do fall through the cracks, people for whom there is no safety net in our society. For these people, there is only the help of God and the mercy of strangers, strangers like you and like me. When God sings a song of the needfulness of others, we must be sure to hear it.

The "Prayer of St. Francis" was written early in the twentieth century, but it has always seemed to me to be an excellent reminder of God's expectation of God's children in the world.

Lord, make me an instrument of your peace,
Where there is hatred, let me sow love;
*   where there is injury, pardon;*
*   where there is doubt, faith;*
*   where there is despair, hope;*
*   where there is darkness, light;*
*   where there is sadness, joy;*
O Divine Master, grant that I may not so much
*   seek to be consoled as to console;*
*   to be understood as to understand;*
*   to be loved as to love.*
For it is in giving that we receive;
*   it is in pardoning that we are pardoned;*
*   and it is in dying that we are born to eternal life.*

A Song of Renewal

"We're sorry to tell you this..." What a horrible phrase to hear in the hospital! It always prefaces really bad news. There was a young man who was brought in by helicopter from the northern area close to Duluth. He had been in a tavern brawl and had been kicked in the head. His buddies took him to the local ER, where they wanted to admit him but being a typical immortal young man, he refused. He went home with his friends. Later, when they couldn't wake him up they called an ambulance, and he was transferred to our trauma center and the CCU.

The friends said he had no family. The brain surgeon who worked with him was gravely worried about the injuries; after 24 hours with little or no brain activity we all assumed that they would be making a decision to discontinue life support. During that time, diligent searching turned up a foster brother, then a blood aunt, then a sister.

These young people were a product of the system. Parents who dealt drugs, kids placed in foster care in their early teens. They were on their own at 18, with no skills, no network of family and friends. They worked minimum wage jobs, crashed wherever they could find a mattress, and drifted through life getting into trouble.

What shall we do? Dustin is going to die, isn't he? What can we do? The doctors and chaplains spent a lot of time with the family members explaining the situation and the ever-decreasing chance of survival. Then the question was posed, "Was Dustin an organ donor? Did he have the little sticker on his driver's license? Had he ever talked about it?" After initial tears and head shaking, the family really rallied and asked good questions about organ donation. "What happens? How do we know he is really brain dead? What if he isn't, what happens then? What happens when we take him off the ventilator and IVs? Will he be in pain? Will he know?"

They finally agreed to let the organ procurement team make its assessment. These people are the most respectful, gentlest, most caring professionals I have ever seen. They are unobtrusive, staying in the back ground, aware that the very sight of them upsets family members. But these special people are the ones who make life possible for so many nameless suffering souls- those who wait years, often in vain, for a second chance at life. They wait for the generosity of families or dying patients themselves to give a kidney, a liver, a heart, a pancreas, a precious organ that will transform them from being near death to starting a new life.

So we watched while Dustin was removed from life support. We waited the hours until his heart stopped beating, the brainwaves flattened out to nothing. We mourned the young man whose life had been so short and so sad. We gave thanks for the gift of life that this tragedy provided to eight people who waited desperately for the phone to ring. "We have a kidney for you! We have a liver for your Dad! We have a heart for your daughter!"

Dustin's sister asked me, "Dustin really made a difference, didn't he? He saved someone's life, didn't he?" From death to new life, we live the Paschal Mystery each day, from dying to rising. With the grace of God.

In the bulb there is a flower; in the seed, an apple tree;
In cocoons, a hidden promise: butterflies will soon be free!
In the cold and snow of winter
*   there's a spring that waits to be,*
Unrevealed until its season, something God alone can see.

(In the Bulb There is a Flower,
Natalie Sleeth, 1986, © Hope Publishing)

A Song of Providence

Every year for eight years, I looked forward to a women's retreat experience offered by another area hospital. In early October we would board a passenger bus and travel to an area in the far north called the Boundary Waters Canoe Area, a wild rugged forest filled with lakes and rivers.

We stayed at the famous Gunflint Lodge on the Gunflint Trail, where serious fishermen and canoe enthusiasts came to experience the primitive life, mostly unchanged since the days of the earliest settlers. We came to taste the quiet of the forest and lake, the gourmet meals of their world famous chef, and enjoy the company of good friends. The not so rustic cabins that we booked had all the amenities, including a hot tub for six close companions.

During our visits we hiked many miles and often stopped at the outfitters down the road, at the very end of the Gunflint Trail. The owners were big city dropouts, an architect and his designer wife from Chicago who had grown tired of the city lifestyle and longed for the peace of nature. They had sold their home, and had purchased the outfitter business from the previous owners (who wanted to retire somewhere warm!). They were avid canoe and kayak people who had vacationed in the area for years. We would visit with them and wish them the best.

That was October. In late January, back at the hospital, I was called to the Emergency Room in the evening. The day had been filled with admissions from car accidents due to heavy snowfall and icy roads. As I entered the ER, the triage nurse told me that a patient had come in with his wife who was terrified and in need of moral support and prayer. I introduced myself and asked her to fill me in on what she knew. It sometimes helps people to talk about what is happening.

She told me they were traveling to Chicago, some six hours from us, to attend a wedding. She said they made the trip often from upper Minnesota and always stopped in our city as it was a good resting point. They always stayed at the same "Mom and Pop" motel. They had checked in early last night, had dinner, and gone to bed. In the morning her husband said he had an awful headache and just needed a few more hours rest. She went out to get breakfast; when she came back he said the headache had gotten worse. She gave him a common pain reliever and read her book for an hour or so. When she woke him again, he told her that he needed to go to the hospital, something was terribly wrong. She called the front desk and the owner told her that our hospital was just down the road. Then, like the Good Samaritan in Scripture, he loaded the couple in his car and drove them to the ER.

The patient was seen immediately and taken for tests which showed that he was suffering from a brain aneurysm. Our hospital, at that time, had in residence a world famous neurosurgeon, who recommended immediate surgery to relieve the pressure and stop the bleeding. I stayed with her until he was returned to the Intensive Care Unit. We arranged for her to have a private place to sleep in the hospital, near the ICU. She had no family to call. The motel owner brought her luggage, promised to deliver her car, and asked what else she needed. She was overwhelmed with the kindness shown to her.

When I returned to work the next day, I stopped in to see her. He was doing much better, though still was in Critical Care. She told me that they had seriously talked about driving straight through to Chicago this trip, and how she was so grateful that they had chosen to stop. "What if this had happened on the road? What if we had been at home, so far from medical help?" So, of course, I asked, "Where do you live?"

"Oh, we live way up north, almost an hour past Grand Marais, at the very end of the Gunflint Trail on the Boundary Waters Canoe Area."

I was so surprised, and so were they, when I told them about our annual trip to Gunflint Lodge, and our recent visit to their outfitters business! We talked about the way things in life seem to weave together, bringing us in contact with one another in the most unusual of circumstances. And how the kindness of strangers can sometimes make all the difference in the world.

They are still living in the North Country, on the border with Canada, enjoying the fishing, the canoeing, the moose and the loons. He is alive because God led them to stop in the right place at the right time, where the care of strangers—and unknown friends—would mean the difference between life and death.

Be not dismayed whate'er betide, God will take care of you!
Beneath His wings of love abide, God will take care of you!
God will take care of you, through every day o'er all the way;
He will take care of you; God will take care of you!

(Be Not Dismayed, Civilla Durfee Martin, 1866-1948)

A Song of Hunger

One would think that Sundays for a chaplain working at a hospital would be a natural thing; kind of an extension of regular Sunday worship. The dynamic in a hospital is much different. For patients, Sundays are big visiting days. Unless no one comes.

One early spring Sunday morning, I was working on the day shift. It was pretty quiet when I checked into the office and sat down at my desk to review the night log. I thought I might write some condolence cards, maybe clean up the pile of paper on my desk, when my pager started to vibrate.

Most chaplains, indeed most hospital employees who wear pagers, have them set to audible rings or tones. Unfortunately, my hearing had deteriorated to the point where I can't tell if my pager is going off, or if my ears are just ringing! So I set mine to vibrate and give off a low grade buzz, kind of like the battery is ready to die. But for me it works.

I checked the pager number. Emergency room! I hurried down the hall hoping no one was too terribly hurt. As I walked in the double doors, the charge nurse looked up from her computer screen and gave me a big smile of relief.

"Oh good, you're here!" she said. "I have two little boys here who need some TLC and some food. Do you have time?", she asked with an anxious note in her voice.

"I always have time," I replied, not knowing who was

around, who was listening.

She took me to ER 10, where two worried little boys were sitting quietly in the corner. Dad was in the bed talking with two police officers and a security guard. His replies to their questions were disjointed and rambling. Then I noticed that he was restrained and both officers were armed.

"Can I take these young men for some breakfast?" I asked in as cheery a voice as I could muster. "Hey, guys, someone told me that you might be hungry. Is that true?"

The boys looked up at me, and their faces lost some of the strained look. "Well, yeah, we're hungry," the older boy said. His little brother looked at him and then at me and echoed the words, "Yeah, we're hungry."

I asked their father if it was ok to take them with me, including the police officers in the request. "Sure, sure..." Dad's reply faded off. Then he looked at me and asked, "Is your name Mary? I need a person named Mary. I will only give my wallet to someone named Mary. Are you Mary?"

Actually my name is a variation of Mary and I assured him that my name means Mary in another language. That was good enough for him. He very willingly reached into his pocket and handed over the wallet, which the police officers had been asking him for.

This man was on medication for a mental condition, but had not been taking it and had slipped into an extreme state of mental confusion. Unfortunately, in his dementia he had loaded up his two sons in his truck and broken into his employer's premises, setting off burglar alarms. The police arrived and apprehended him and, of course, the two boys. They were trying to identify him and not cause trauma to the children.

I gave the wallet to security, reassured Dad that I would take good care of his boys and gathered them up. I chattered brightly about how neat it was for me to have late breakfast with two handsome young men. I kept talking all the way to the cafeteria, telling the boys about my grandchildren and how much I missed having them around. They were giggling and laughing by the time we reached the hospital cafeteria.

It seems they had not eaten since supper the night before, so we loaded up their tray with fruit and sandwich material and chocolate milk. While they were eating, they calmly said, "Dad didn't take his medicine, so he gets sick then." No comment about police or alarms. They were very nice little guys, caught up in a world they had no part in creating. Before I handed them over to their tearful aunt—"She's our best aunt!"— I told them if they were ever in trouble or needed help, they could always come here, to Sacred Heart. A chaplain would always be present, if not me then another chaplain. And they would always be welcomed. And fed.

Whatsoever you do to the least of my brothers that you do unto me.
When I was hungry you gave me to eat.
When I was thirsty you gave me to drink.
Now enter into the home of My Father.
(Willard Jabusch, © 1966, OCP Publications)

A Song of Comfort

There is a ministry out there in the world, a grass roots effort, called Threshold Singing. Small groups of caring people gather together at the bedside of folks who are terminally ill or dying, and sing songs of comfort and hope written to help them as they stand on the Threshold of a new life.

The songs are many and varied. Some are old standards and others are specially written for the journey. So many times when I was with a patient who was very sick or within hours of dying, the singing of songs brought comfort to the one dying and often to the family gathered there.

There was a delightful lady who had struggled for years with COPD (chronic obstructive pulmonary disorder). She had a devoted son who cared for her lovingly and with good humor and a positive attitude. Her disease progressed over a period of 2 to 3 years, causing her to be hospitalized often. Whenever I saw she was a patient, I would make an extra effort just to stop in and say hello. One evening she came in by ambulance in great distress. She was admitted to the Critical Care Unit, and the doctors told her son that this time she wouldn't be going home. There was just no more fight in her. He was so sad and tearful, holding my hand, holding her hand and telling her how much he loved her. He wanted to go and make some calls to close family so that they could see her before it was too late, but he was reluctant to leave her. I promised him I would stay until he returned.

I asked if I could sing to her quietly. I had sung songs for her lots of times before. With his permission I started singing songs I knew she liked...the old standards like Amazing Grace, How Great Thou Art, and In the Garden. I also sang a "going away" song from Threshold singers called From My Heart to Your Heart. It tells how hearts speak to one another, how we can comfort one another with our life song, and how we are able to bless each other even when one of us goes where the other one cannot.

I didn't realize that her son was standing on the other side of the privacy curtain. When I was done he came around to me and hugged me close as we both cried for his loss. He thanked me for caring enough to sing to his beloved mother and for caring for him.

I saw a poster one time that said, "Sing like no one is listening, Dance like no one is watching." That's good advice.

From my heart to your heart a song without end.
May it offer you comfort and healing my friend.
Though I cannot go with you your journey goes on.
I can laugh with you, cry with you,
    sing till you've won your freedom from suffering,
    release from all fear.
May you find all the love that you needed was here.
                              (Maria Culberson, A Threshold Song)

Helen's Songs

As Song of Persistence

Daniel Levitin wrote a great book titled This is Your Brain on Music *(Plume Books, 2006) that details (among other things) the physical interactions of the various parts of the brain when a person is "doing" music. One thing he says is that practice is more important than talent when seeking musical expertise.*

But learning to do something new gets harder as I get older. I guess there are lots of valid reasons for that, but it doesn't seem fair. I'm fortunate that I learned to "do" music very young, because it was much easier then. Whether it was singing different styles and languages, playing the piano, learning to read music (which is a foreign language, too!), it's all easier when you're young. But you still have to practice.

In college I was enrolled in a Bachelor of Music in Education degree program. It was comprehensive, to say the least: vocal, band, orchestra, and classroom music, K-12. It was impossible to fulfill all of the requirements in the usual eight semesters; I went to summer school, too.

The summer between my freshman and sophomore years I made the ridiculous decision to take applied music (that's the fancy name for lessons) in piano, voice and flute. That meant spending four or more hours a day in a practice room. An un-air-conditioned room. In the summer. It was grueling, but I enjoyed it in a perverse way; I was suffering for my art.

Towards the end of the summer I was playing a French piece for my flute lesson. It was long, difficult, and beautiful. I remember the sweat dripping off my nose as I poured my heart into it. My instructor looked at me, pursed his lips and said, "Well, you're not a hack anymore." What did he mean by that, I asked, ready to be mad and defend myself.

"You played that like a musician. You're not just playing the notes, you're making music." He smirked a little self-satisfied smile that told me he considered it all to his credit, not mine. Maybe more than some of it was his doing, but I was the one who had sweated through the practice sessions, so I pursed my lips back at him and turned to the next piece.

Twenty years later I decided to study organ in graduate school. Dr. Miller, my blessed instructor of infinite patience and wisdom, required two hours a day of practice, seven days a week. It was definitely cooler in the organ practice rooms (in fact, I often had to wear my winter hat and coat) but even more demanding of my decades-older self.

Playing the organ not only requires the manual dexterity of a very good pianist but the bi-pedal flexibility of a circus acrobat. Well, maybe not that much, but your feet have to dance over a three-octave pedalboard at the same time as your hands are flitting over the keyboards (yes, plural, at least two and often three or four). For months I did pedal exercises, learning to play scales with my toes and heels. I practiced hymns, starting with simple ones that only required your feet to play three or four dif-

ferent notes. But you had to find the notes without looking at your feet. For months, it seemed an impossible task.

One of the pieces I practiced constantly was The Old Hundredth Doxology, a weekly response in the church service, dating back to the Genevan Psalter of the 16th century. It has a tricky pedal part, so I included it at the end of every practice session, determined to play it eventually for church. Late one evening as I wrapped up my practicing for the night, thinking about what I needed to do the next day, I realized that I was playing it. I could literally feel the new neural pathways firing in my brain as my feet seemed to have a guidance system of their own. I played it again. And again. It was a critical turning point in my organ playing.

There are always challenges in life. Some we present to ourselves, some are given to us. Sometimes it takes us longer to figure out our response, but if we persist, if we practice, our brains, our bodies and our spirits somehow learn what we need to know to overcome the difficulties and meet the challenge. We are always better off for the efforts.

Praise God from whom all blessings flow,
Praise God, all creatures here below.
Praise God above, ye heavenly host.
Praise Father, Son and Holy Ghost.

A Song for Everyone

There's a line from the musical "Wicked" that says, "Everyone deserves the chance to fly." That has settled in my heart, reinforcing a long-held belief that everyone deserves the chance to sing, to let their voice fly. Because singing is like breathing for me, it was difficult at first for me to understand how or why that would not be the same for everyone. It not only should be; it can be.

I met my husband, Dear One, through mutual friends. In the small town where we lived, it was pretty much impossible not to know everyone, at least in passing, and we had been to the same gatherings a few times over the past few years. Our "yenta" (Italian, but a yenta none-the-less) was a good friend to both of us. She pretty much forced him to call me and invite me to join a group of acquaintances going out for dinner. I accepted, and within minutes of sitting down at the table, we were mutually intrigued and within hours knew that we were meant for each other.

A few weeks later, he attended church with me. I was directing the choir at a Lutheran church, so we went to a service where I didn't have to "work." That way we could sit together, along with my three boys. The opening hymn was almost a deal breaker. Although he sang with gusto and resonance, he had absolutely no sense of pitch! It was nothing short of painful for me. Even the kids, who all sing quite well, looked at him in...awe. As in awe-ful.

After the service, we went to my house and I said, "Look, I love you and all, but if I'm going to sit next to you in church for the rest of my life, you have to learn to sing." He was aware of his shortcomings (his mother had frequently pointed out the problem) and was somewhat sensitive to it because his father had been a fine singer. But Dear One believed sincerity made up for it when it came to singing hymns. It may level the balance a bit, but...

I sat him down next to me at the piano, and we spent about 45 minutes learning to match pitches. Another few sessions and his lovely baritone voice entered into conversation with his ears to produce an excellent singer. It's not easy for him, even now, but he leads the singing in church with the same gusto and resonance, and with the correct melody. He's even learned to sing harmony with the choir when needed.

I've repeated that process many times with others who either don't sing accurately or were told they couldn't/shouldn't sing. No one should ever be told that they cannot or should not sing. Don't ever let anyone tell you not to sing. Unless there is a physical impairment with one's ears or vocal apparatus, anyone can learn to sing. It is part of our humanity, part of our very brain; as important as the drive to communicate with words is the urge to communicate with song, to let your voice soar in joy or sorrow, in praise of God or celebration of life.

Everyone deserves the chance to fly.

My life goes on in endless song
    above earth's lamentations,
I hear the soft though far-off sound
    that hails a new creation.
No storm can shake my inmost calm
    while to that rock I'm clinging.
Since Christ is Lord of heaven and earth,
    how can I keep from singing?

(How Can I Keep From Singing, Robert Lowry, 1826-1899)

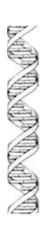

A Song of Faith

Within a year of marrying, we moved to Colorado. Dear One was to be in charge of the construction and operation of a woods product facility. It was a step up in the business, and a wonderful place to live. We bought a beautiful large house, just blocks from the golf course. We learned to downhill and cross country ski, and worked and played equally hard.

But the business world can be fickle, and after three years, he was out of a job, with a wife, a house, three kids and a dog. I had my own music business but it was not terribly lucrative, so he went to work in a small cabinet-making shop. It was physically hard work, and he worked nights sometimes. His hands grew tough from the splinters, his arms and back muscles grew stronger, and he made a difference in the success of the company by streamlining production and sharing his knowledge of the materials. Mentally, he was bored to tears.

One afternoon, we ate lunch in silence as he prepared to go to work. "I don't know how much longer I can do this," he finally said. "We need to think about maybe moving back to Wisconsin. I can certainly get a job there."

We discussed several possibilities, but somehow it felt like stepping backwards.

I asked him, "If you could do anything at all, what would you do?" Without hesitation, he said, "I'd be a minister."

"Really? Well, why don't you do that?" Naiveté is such a love-

ly thing. He looked at me as if he were thinking just that.

"We have a house, three kids, and a dog. How could we do that?" He was more practical, I guess.

"Well, I don't know. We'll figure something out." And we did.

Several months later we gave the house back to the bank, sold most of its contents, and loaded up the rest in a 22-foot moving truck. Like a wagon train, I followed the moving truck with the big Dodge van, towing a camper and carrying a canoe, and we set out for Bangor, Maine, where there was a seminary that specialized in small church ministry.

We arrived after a few weeks (having visited our way across the country) with $500 and no jobs. The "student housing" was a tiny apartment, less than a third the size of our Colorado home. We looked at it and cried. What on earth had we done?

But the piano fit in the corner, and the stereo went beside it. The kids were crowded and the weather was cold, but there were other kids there, too. The books went on the unheated porch; our bed fit even if you couldn't open the bedroom door all the way. The kitchen was like the camper, kind of, if you thought about it that way. And Stephen King lived three blocks away, how cool is that? It was Labor Day weekend and school—for Dear One as well as the children—started the following Tuesday. So did the rest of our lives.

Here I am Lord, is it I, Lord?
I have heard you calling in the night.
I will go Lord, if you lead me.
I will hold your people in my heart.

(Here I Am, Lord, Dan Schutte, ©1981 OCP Publications)

A Song of Patient Waiting

"Do you want to go to a football game?" Jay asked the week before I was to visit her in chilly Michigan.

"A what?"

"A football game, a high school game. A few of my church kids are in the band and I told them I would go to the half-time show."

"Okay, sure." I tried to be enthusiastic. I'd "been there, done that" in high school, and it's cold in November in Michigan, but I was amenable. Sort of.

"And Chris will be going with us."

I knew a much longer conversation was about to take place.

Jay had been my roommate for two years in graduate school in Boston. I was a "non-traditional" student; that means I was older than most of my fellow/sister students by about 20 years. The course load required that I stay in Boston three or four days each week, so I had a room in the Theology House.

Jay was almost exactly the age of my oldest son, but we had a lot in common. We were in the same degree program, we both played flute and were studying organ, and we were both a little OCD about school. Jay had earned the money for grad school by working on her father's farm, and I do mean working. For two years after her college graduation she did the hard labor of farming: crops, animals, the whole picture. She wasn't about to waste her time or money. She dated occasionally, but most of the guys were pretty immature compared to her. Many late-night conversations centered about her belief, with which I agreed, that God would bring the right person to her at the right time.

After graduation she went to serve as music minister at a church in the mid-west while I continued with doctoral work. We stayed in close touch. Over the next few years she thought more and more about marrying and having a family. But she was still pretty particular about male friends, and she was serving in a church leadership role that wasn't really conducive to partying. Her faith in God's providence was unwavering, but sometimes she worried that she wasn't meant to find Mister Right.

By then I was beginning my dissertation research, and her church agreed to take part in it. I made plans to spend a few days with her while I interviewed people. That's when the football game conversation took place.

She explained that she had met a guy online, on a Christian website, and this would be their first face-to-face meeting. They had spent hours and hours on the telephone and exchanged emails. They shared religious convictions, social concerns, likes and dislikes. He was several years older, different from the "boys" she had dated. I would be the chaperone, and ready to provide a good excuse to split early if things didn't turn out well.

When Chris came over to Jay's little house, he and I chatted while she did some last minute things. He was pleasant, attractive, and polite, and I decided he was perfect for her. We drove *over to the high school, and as Jay and I walked behind him to the field, I whispered in her ear, "You be nice to him. He's definitely a keeper!" and made a totally inappropriate comment about his butt. She laughed. I nearly froze my nose off at that game.*

They got married, of course. Within a few years she had four beautiful boys, including twins. She is a beautiful, Godly woman who cares for her family in every way. She still works with church music, and teaches piano along with homeschooling her boys. She sings to them all the time, of course, and they sing back. She and Chris have built a home firmly based on their faith in God, who they know gives all good things in God's own time.

I sing because I'm happy. I sing because I'm free,
for His eye is on the sparrow, and I know he watches me.

(His Eye is on the Sparrow, Civilla D. Martin,1905)

A Song of Siblings

Our brother George died on Moira's birthday.

He was living in Georgia, near our parents, and had begun to resolve a lot of the issues he and Dad had been struggling with all of George's life. He was the oldest child, the only son, and of course Mom doted on him. She had been hard on him when he was a kid, but we knew he was her favorite. He broke her heart more than once, but that didn't matter. He was Bucky.

His health was not good; he had heart trouble and didn't really take care of himself. He was a kind, caring, "take in the strays" type of guy. I remember we happened to be at our parents' house once when I was about 35 years old. He walked in and looked at me and said, "Baby sister! I wouldn't have recognized you if I'd passed you on the street!"

"Well, you goof, look in the mirror! How could you not?" We turned toward the big mirror that hung over the sofa, and our eyes met in the reflections. The same nose, the same smile, the same round face stared back at us.

"Huh. Look at that. Dad, got any beer?"

Several years later, Dear One and I and the kids had just gotten home from a trip to Michigan, literally walked into the house with our suitcases, when the phone rang. It was Mom, telling us that Bucky had had a heart attack. He had been at home, sitting on the couch with his step-sons, watching TV. According to one of them, he just sat up a bit and said, "Jeez, my heart stopped."

He looked at the boys and said, "I love you guys." And died. His sons called the EMTs and their mother, but there was nothing to be done.

Mom and Dad were devastated. They behaved in ways I would never have believed. Grief can be so overwhelming. Neither of them ever really got over it. Dad carried guilt for the issues they had not resolved; Mom just grieved to the depths of her heart and soul.

Of course, we went to Georgia immediately, Moira from Wisconsin, me from Massachusetts. The funeral was quickly arranged at the "family" funeral home and church. I sang at the cemetery, Precious Lord, Take My Hand. I wrote my own third verse, one that emphasized light and life instead of darkness and death. People have asked me how I could do that without "losing it." It was my last gift to George. I wanted to give a message of hope, life, and resurrection to his weeping children and wife, to our parents, to the rest of the family. I could, for a change, sing my brother to sleep.

Now the path appears and the light shines clear,
For the night is past and gone.
At the River I stand, guide my feet to that land.
Take my hand, precious Lord, lead me home.

(*Precious Lord, Take My Hand*
Thomas Andrew Dorsey, 1938)

A Song of Promise

Alzheimer's had been sneaking up on Dad for several years. When we finally all moved to Florida—Mom, Dad, Dear One, and me—it was a bit more obvious. We lived in a duplex, a beautiful new house for two families, with a pool across the back, palm trees in the yard, and lots of garden space for Mom's green thumb.

Over about three years he faded away, into the past most of the time. He would swim in the pool every day, and afterwards he would sit by the pool, talking to himself and gesturing. He was, Dear One explained, putting his life in order in preparation for the end. But, boy, was he stubborn about that end!

During the last week his body began to shut down bit by bit. His mind, when he was lucid, was very aware of the embarrassments he endured as he lost control of bodily functions. Mom was overwhelmed by the whole thing. Losing her companion of more than 60 years was more than she could contemplate, I think. She stayed back, allowing me and my brother's widow, Rose, to take care of Dad.

His last weekend, he wouldn't sit down or go to sleep. "Terminal restlessness" is the descriptor, but Dad took it to excess. He kept saying, "I have to get out of here. I have to go." We asked him, "Where do you want to go?"

"I don't know, but I have to go now. I have to go somewhere." All day Friday, he would sit down in his red leather recliner,

which had for a few years been his chair in daytime and bed at night, but he would remain only for a few minutes and then would be up again. He used a walker (when we reminded him!) and went back and forth from the front door to the back patio doors. Rose was exhausted from following him around and taking care of Mom, so after dinner I sent her to bed.

He finally stopped for a few hours about 10 p.m., not sleeping, but not moving around. I started gently to rub the back of his neck, singing "Oh, What a Beautiful Morning" from Oklahoma, one of his favorites that he would sing himself many mornings. It didn't seem right under the circumstances, though, so I switched to hymns, mostly humming.

We were seated facing the patio doors, looking out at the pool with the moon reflecting on the water. It was dark in the house, to encourage sleep, I hoped. At one point he said softly, "Who are those people?"

"What people? Where?" I asked.

"Those three people standing there. Are they waiting for me?" He seemed almost asleep.

"Well, I don't know. Maybe they are. Maybe it's your Mom, and George, and Amados." Amados had been a father figure to him, a protector many times from the abuse of his own father, and the source of his self-value from childhood.

"Hmmp. Maybe it is."

I gently told him it would be okay to go with them. But he was silent. I took advantage of his calmness to crawl on the couch and immediately fell asleep.

I was awakened at 5:30 am by his struggles to get up from the chair. I took him to the bathroom, let the dog out, did the usual morning things. His restlessness increased as the day went on. "I have to get out of here. I have to go."

We gave him the anti-anxiety medications, the morphine, anything to get him to rest. By 10 pm that night we were all exhausted! The hospice nurse came about midnight and gave him enough meds to "knock out a racehorse," but it didn't even slow him down. He locked himself in the bathroom about 2 am, causing the nurse and me to go into gales of laughter. "I've never had a patient lock me out before!" she said, wiping tears from her eyes.

I found a key, brought him out and got him seated again, and started to sing, gently rubbing his neck again, just a feathery touch. "Teach me, grandmother, for I am just a child, and I've wandered from the path that I was walking. Can I run to you? Can I lay my burden down? Can I sit by your fire and listen?" And he stayed still as long as I sang that song. All night. As long as I sang.

By 7 am, the transport that the hospice nurse had requested to take him to the Hospice House, where they hoped to be able to manage his meds better, arrived, and I helped him into a wheelchair. The attendants took him out to the transport and locked the chair down, and I climbed into the front passenger seat.

"Okay, Dad, we're going now. You wanted to go, so here we

go," I said cheerfully, as if we were setting out on a great adventure. He opened his eyes, looked down the road before him, and smiled. His eyes closed and remained that way as we made the 20-minute trip.

He got settled into a room, while I went to work (just a few blocks away, fortunately) and arranged with Rose and Mom to meet them there at 11 am. They were ready early, and Mom was anxious to go. They arrived just before 10; he had died minutes before.

The nurse told us that they had washed and shaved him, "gotten him all ship-shape," and by the time she came back to the room from disposing of the towels and things, he was gone.

I'm convinced that he didn't want to die in their home. He didn't want Mom to have that memory in her house. That's why he had to "get out of there." I'm glad I had those last hours to sing him closer to where he wanted to go. I know he's enjoying every Beautiful Morning with Grandma, George, and Amados, and Mom, too.

Oh, what a beautiful morning! Oh, what a beautiful day!
I got a beautiful feeling, everything's going my way.

(Oh, What a Beautiful Morning,
Oscar Hammerstein II, © 1943 Williamson Music)

Moira's Songs

Part Two

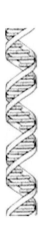

A Song of Service

During my time as a chaplain I was blessed and privileged to work for Fr. Lawrence Dunklee, a nationally recognized figure in ethics and morality, and an especially gifted speaker. Fr. Dunklee organized a training session for area churches that wanted to develop their own home and hospital visitation teams. The last session was a round table discussion with some of us chaplains there to answer questions. The inevitable question was, "Why did you choose to do this kind of work?" In my case I could hardly say that God had caused Sr. Augusta to call me after I complained to Him! So I used one of the hymns that is popular today in Catholic Liturgy, "Will You Let Me Be Your Servant?"

Will you let me be your servant? Let me be as Christ to you?
Pray that I may have the grace to let you be my servant too.
Richard Gillard (1977)

That is what pastoral care is all about—walking with another on whatever road his or her journey follows, reminding them that they are not alone: Jesus walks with them too.

Only three years later Fr. Dunklee, faced with esophageal cancer, told me how hard it was to let others care for him. He called it the ministry of dependence. He was diagnosed in October and died in January. After years of ministering to others, offering prayer and sacrament to the dying, he had to allow others to minister to him. His life and his death were grace-filled, both for himself and those of us who were privileged to be his servants too.

A Song of Resurrection

September 9, 2013

We buried Father Klimek last week. He was my mentor and my friend, a rock of faith and goodness in a world of fear and suffering.

When I first met him, I knew he was the priest at the hospital who had been there forever. There were so many stories about him; how no matter what time you were brought into the ER Fr. Klimek would show up to pray with you. How he remembered everyone's name and how many kids they had. He had been there so long that some of the younger patients could remember their parents and grandparents talking about him. He officiated at more funerals in town than any other clergy members. He went to nursing homes, to assisted living facilities, in town and outside of town, visiting the sick and elderly, bringing communion and bringing hope. Indeed, the hospital made that their motto: *There Is Hope Here.* We would all laugh to ourselves and say, yeah, that's 'cause Fr. Klimek's there!

If he came to pray with you, the day was better. You felt better. You weren't so frightened. Just by walking into a room he brought a sense of the presence of God.

He was already 75 when I started working there. He was so good to me. He knew I was nervous and unsure. I told him I really didn't feel worthy to be working with him, visiting and praying with patients.

"I'll help you", he said. "Have faith. God called you here, so God will give you what you need each day. We just take things one day at a time, day by day."

When I'd get anxious or frustrated he'd look at me and shake his head, "Day by day, day by day."

He worked all hours of the day and night. He loved being with people, bringing them consolation, bringing them hope, bringing them a taste of God's love.

When he knew he was dying, he didn't want to be alone and he agreed to let us take turns sitting up with him at night. The greatest privilege of my life was the night I sat by his bedside, holding his hand.

"When you get to heaven, would you say nice things to God about me, please?" I asked. He chuckled and squeezed my hand. We had been at the bedside of so many people when they died. He liked for me to pray the 23rd Psalm with him when a patient had passed away. "His goodness and mercy shall follow me all the days of my life and I will dwell in the house of the Lord forever".

We sang at his funeral, all of the songs he had picked out months before. Beginning with *Be Not Afraid* and ending with *On Eagles' Wings:*

And he shall raise you up, on eagles' wings,
bear you on the breath of dawn,
make you to shine like the sun,
and hold you in the palm of his hand."

(Michael Joncas © 1979 OCP)

I miss him so much.

Swing low, sweet chariot, coming for to carry him home,
swing low, sweet chariot, coming for to carry him home.
If you get to heaven before I do,
    coming for to carry me home,
    tell all my friends I'm a-coming too,
    coming for to carry me home.

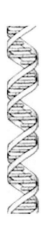

Helen's Songs

Part Two

A Song of Laughter

During the five years that Dear One was working as a hospice chaplain, he rarely "brought his work home." He would occasionally share with me stories about an interesting person he'd met, like the woman who was great friends with a famous football coach, or the famous writer's father who was facing the end of a tumultuous life. Many of the hospice patients suffered from dementia, but some "kept their marbles" right up to the end.

One of those was Beatrice, a stringy, white-haired little terror of 94 years, who kept the nurses and caregivers at bay by being demanding, critical, and unsmiling. But few can resist the charm of Dear One, and he cannot resist a challenge. It took him just a few visits to establish a rapport with her. He validated her ill-temper as justified by her circumstances, but pointed out that she also could make the situation better if she used a different approach. Grudgingly, she let him sit for a bit as he drew her story out of her. Everyone likes to talk about themselves.

He learned that she loved music, especially dancing, and knew a lot of the songs from the '30s and '40s. "I wrote a song, you know," she said one day. "It was a poem at first, but it should be a song. But I can't write music or nothin'."

"My wife's a musician, maybe she can write it for you," he volunteered. So he took an old cassette recorder from home and had her recite her poem. He wrote down what he heard her say,

*just to make sure it was correct and clear, and brought it all to
me.*

> Ain't asked you to love me, couldn't care less.
>> It's your laughter that haunts me.
>> Would you also confess,
>> it's better by far than the sharing of bodies,
>> or a trip to the bar.
> Ain't asked you to love me, couldn't care less.
> It's your laughter that haunts me,
>> would you also confess?
> We'll walk in sunshine and we'll walk in shade,
>> loving the moments our laughter has made.

*I've always said that when I write a song I can't take any
credit for it. "The angel of music sings songs in my head," as Andrew Lloyd Weber said in* Phantom of the Opera. *It's just there,
and my job is to write it down. Her poem became a 1940s torch
song that I wrote out quite quickly and then recorded on the
same cassette player to take back to her.*

*I wanted to be sure she liked it, so we went to the facility to-
gether. The aura of sadness that sometimes permeates nursing
homes can be somehow...diminishing, making me feel smaller,
less real, less human. But the look on Beatrice's face when she
heard her song relieved that completely. "Not bad for an old lady,
is it?" she grinned. We assured her it was definitely hit material,
and left her the cassette and player.*

*She died about three months later. I hope she's walking
in sunshine with the one whose loving laughter was with her till
the end.*

Ain't asked you to love me, couldn't care less.
It's your laughter that haunts me,
    I must also confess.

A Song of Sisters: a Duet

Moira

For most of their lives, Mom and Dad seemed to deal well with the frequent—sometimes annual—relocations required of military life. You simply receive orders and you pack up and move to a new place. But they were gypsies at heart, because after Dad retired they still moved. They didn't sell the house in Jacksonville when he was transferred to Connecticut, knowing it would only be a few years until he would retire, they would move back and that would be home.

But work was very hard to find. He traveled over 50 miles each way for nearly a year before they decided...to move. And so it continued for the next 25 years: from Florida to Eau Claire, Wisconsin, then north to Superior, back to Eau Claire; down to St. Petersburg, Florida, east to Arcadia, Florida (where Mom and I were born) and then, out of the blue, to rural southern Georgia. Even though they lived there longer than anyplace else (17 years all together), even there, they sold their first house in the woods and moved into town. Dad was 85 when they decided on one last move.

For years I had begged them to come north and live with us, but the bitterly cold winters kept them away. But when Helen's husband was called to serve a church in southwest Florida, Mom and Dad announced that they would move there, too. Realizing that they could no longer do everything themselves, Dad suggested that the four of them purchase a twin home (also called a duplex) together. God provided an ideal, newly constructed house, and the miracle of coordinating buying, selling and moving two households 1700 miles apart was somehow accomplished.

Helen

Mom had always had complex medical problems including breast cancer, bypass surgery, internal organ issues and finally back problems. All of them seem to require extra surgeries, protracted recovery and complications. Like many of the elderly, her calendar was filled with doctor appointments. We had our hands full, ferrying the parents back and forth while trying to fulfill our responsibilities at work and church.

Moira

When your parents are in their final years and living far away, it is challenging to be present to them in a significant way. I felt inadequate since I could not physically help. So I would call Mom and Dad every few days, checking in, offering news and moral support. Often the calls ended after just a few minutes with Mom saying, "Don't run up your phone bill." I tried explaining that long distance charges were not an issue especially in these days of unlimited calls. I talked with Helen often, offering her thanks and appreciation, and would come and visit as often as possible. Helen found it so helpful to be able to share the events, decisions, and difficulties, and was appreciative of my support, even as the majority of the caregiver role fell on her.

Helen

As Dad wandered further and further into the dementia of Alzheimer's, Mom had to take more responsibility for his care. And she didn't like it. Over the years, they had taken turns being "patient" and "nurse," but mostly he had taken care of her. He pampered her and waited on her. When she was in rehab following a particularly nasty back surgery, he worked day and night to keep the house clean, the laundry done, the plants cared for, and the dog walked. He would go to visit her and between the heat of the nursing home and the opportunity to sit down in a comfy rocking chair, he would often fall asleep.

When it became apparent that some in-home help would be needed, Mom seemed to like the idea of having someone do the household chores (at least the ones she didn't enjoy) and help out with the cooking. She wasn't happy about the expense. After running through three or four different "granny nannies", she agreed to pay George's widow, Rose, to come from New York state and assist with Dad in his last months. Dad hated having what he called "all those bossy women" telling him what to do. Mom happily turned all that over to Rose, and distanced herself as much as possible.

Moira

After Dad died, Mom quickly thanked Rose, gave her some money and sent her on her way. She repainted the house and tried to end any extended care suggestions. Her back problems were exacerbated by a number of falls, and her mobility decreased as her pain increased. She finally agreed to have daily companions, two women from Helen's church with whom she became friends. Just about two years after Dad's passing, she fell again, and was in terrible pain.

Helen

We scheduled surgery just before Christmas to repair the damage to her back. Afterwards, her surgeon sat with his head in his hands and explained sadly that there was far more damage to the bones than could have been caused by the fall. Biopsies and a bone scan confirmed that the breast cancer had metastasized to her bones and it was progressing quickly.

Moira

She refused any radiation or chemo treatment, remembering the misery that she had suffered following her breast cancer and mastectomy. Helen arranged for hospice care for pain management, installed a nursery monitor so that she could hear Mom at night, and kept her as comfortable as possible. As January progressed so did her condition. She spent much of her time sleeping. I called daily, talking to Mom when she was able. Some days she felt better but she was going steadily downhill.

Helen

Moira's birthday is in February and she planned to be with Mom that week. Mom never liked to think about Moira's birthday because our brother George had died on her 49th birthday, which that year also happened to be Ash Wednesday. Both were days Mom hated to see on the calendar. Her family had too many instances when someone died on the birthday of another close family member. That week was also our aunt's birthday, Mom's sister, who Mom had not wanted to know about her diagnosis or prognosis. It was a difficult week.

Moira flew to Florida with her oldest daughter, Jennifer, who wanted to be with her grandmother and do whatever she could. When they arrived, it was obvious that it would only be a matter of days. Hospice provided palliative care, and we promised her that her pain would be controlled. She would rally intermittently, to talk to Jennifer or my son Daniel when he visited, and she talked to Moira on her birthday. The next day was Ash Wednesday and the lady who had been bringing her communion from church each week also brought ashes.

Moira

I sat with her that night, held her hand, and asked for her forgiveness for anything I might have done to cause hurt. I told her that I forgave her for any hurts over the years. I reminded her that my birthday was over, that Ash Wednesday was over and that her sister's birthday was still a few days away. I told her it was ok for her to go, to find rest, to lay her burdens down. That she had done so well and that we loved her.

Helen

I know that for a time she was kind of mad at me, because somehow I hadn't made the problem go away this time as I had in the past. I had bandaged her injuries, changed her diapers, washed her body, and brushed her hair. I did things I never suspected I could do. I told her every day that I loved her. I knew that she loved me, and was sad to leave her family, her home. But life wasn't fun anymore.

The last evening, the hospice nurse stayed, knowing that it was a matter of hours. She called us just after one in the morning, saying the end was near. Mom died on Thursday, not on anyone's birthday or any special holyday. We were there, and the peace that transformed her face was beyond description. We spent some time, singing a bit, saying good-bye, and then called the funeral home.

Moira

In the front hallway, hanging over Mom's treasured table, was the plaque that had been made for them by a friend in

Georgia, with their names and "est. 1944." They had been married over 60 years. As Helen sat in the kitchen with Nell, the hospice nurse, who had to inventory all of the medications and supplies for hospice, Helen talked about Mom's journey. I was cleaning up in the bedroom, and singing softly to myself. Suddenly we heard a loud crash. Helen looked toward the door and saw that the plaque had fallen, no, jumped, from the wall over the table to land standing up on the floor, leaning against the table legs. "My goodness, what was that?" Nell asked.

"That was Mom. She's saying they don't live here anymore," Helen replied without hesitation. Nell eyed her, thinking that was maybe a little loopy. I walked out of the bedroom and asked what the noise was.

"The name thingy fell off the wall. It didn't even hit the table," Helen told me.

"Oh, that's Mom," I smiled. "She's saying they don't live here anymore."

"Yeah, that's what I said, too." Helen nodded her head, walked over and picked it up. "I don't think I'll hang it back up. It didn't break, and it didn't even scratch the table either."

"Of course not," I said matter-of-factly. "Mom really liked that table. She wouldn't dent it."

Nell was an experienced hospice nurse who preferred working nights. She had been present at many deaths and very little surprised her anymore. She looked at us both, smiled and said, "You're probably right. I've seen some strange things happen."

Helen

At Mom's funeral Moira and her husband sang the final commendation prayer from the Catholic funeral liturgy:

Saints of God, come to her aid.
Come to meet her, angels of the Lord,
receive her soul and present her to God,
present her soul to God Most High.

May Christ who called you, take you home.
May angels lead you to our parents' side.

Receive her soul and present her to God.
Present her soul to God most high.

Give her eternal rest of Lord
and may your light shine down on her forever.
Receive her soul and present her to God,
present her soul to God Most High.

Coda
and More

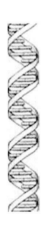

A Bridge to the Next Song

As we were writing our stories from over the years, we marveled that the two little girls who began their LifeSongs by sharing songs at night would grow up to be parts of the same song of service though by different paths. We both knew and experienced life as comforters of the sick. We both knew challenges and sorrows. We both turned to music for solace and comfort; for praise and petition to our loving creator, the Divine Composer.

Now we find that our paths have intersected once more, calling us to sing our songs not only to one another as sisters but to share those songs with all our sisters and brothers. The discovery has given us the strength and courage to begin a new movement in the Symphony. We are following the path that God has shown us. We are offering through retreats, presentations and seminars to share our new understanding of LifeSongs. We hope to help others discover the beauty of their own LifeSongs, to explore the possibilities God presents to each of us, and to add their voices to the Great Symphony.

Alphabetical Index of Songs